Punk P

John Burg

Ravenna Press

History: Collected here for the first time, Punk Poems 01-48 were published in *Punk Poems* (2005) and Punk Poems 49-74 in *Graffito* (2011), both with Ravenna Press; Punk Poems 75-100 as *Vacant* (2022) w/ Scumbag Press, U.K.

Support small presses & independent bookstores.
–jb (punkpoet.net)

Signed First Edition Limited to 125 copies

Cover design by Jack Burgess.

ISBN: 979-8-9890826-8-1
LCCN: 2023945994

ravennapress.com

CONTENTS

To Patsy—

PUNK POEMS

I got nothin' to hide here save desire.

What about it what about it what about it
Oh I'm pissing in a river

All that you desire / Rolls on ahead

–Patti Smith

01

Alternating line of ones & zeros,
Signals, power grids, schematic wires,
Box, blocks, division, quadrant desires,
All arbitrary maps—
The cable between poles
Bouncing outside our window
Click-click-click-click-click
As we lie awake
The house dark & count
Each electron pulse.

02

Talk about the cellular
Level—an electronic search
For coincidence—past lives
Wrapped in coils & networks
Ones & zeros displayed
& out-of-focus
Not believing in connection
Until the knot
Unknots—
Swaggers like a cable.

03

Desire is deciduous, falls away
& buds again—sometimes a cowboy
Brandishes a handgun, French kisses
A Montana redneck w/ a thick grain-
Alcohol tongue—other times
A Tibetan monk tosses flour from
Tall rock monastery walls, powders
Earth w/ possibilities—in time
A wingless crow
Tumbles toward trouble.

04

Bessie Smith sings on Sundays
Pressed, repressed, pressed on
Her voice tired & defiant plays on
In mono on stereo goes on
Moaning & urging
The ring of a church bell resonates on—
Nothing makes this emptiness thing
As good as she does—nothing
Makes you feel any something
Like she does—nothing.

05

In China they take poets seriously—
Arrested Ma Zhe—they know poetry
Can change things can be
A threat to national security—
We forget the risk of paper ideas
Can cause someone to disappear—
Revolution
& renaissance
Start w/ a character—
A brush stroke, a brush fire.

06

He often thinks in brush strokes
& although it's linear
It doesn't travel between 2 points
In a straight line—
Instead it spreads
Folds in on itself—other times
It continues off the paper
Toward something undefined
& never heads
In the direction he expects.

07

Game trails run different terrain
Than highways—
Not hard-wired lines on landscape
Not straight, not inked
Not concerned w/ bends
Or edges—
Paths follow instinct, undulations
Find a way
Between 2 points
On the map or not.

08

As naked as Jim Bridger—like
John Colter oblivious to dangers
Of cause & effect—like Yellowstone tourists
Posing for snapshots w/ park buffalo
Or surveyors dividing & subdividing
Prairies w/ arbitrary lines of barbed
Wire—like widening game trails
To wagon trails to railroad tracks to
4-lane highways w/ neon signs:
LEWIS & CLARK SLEPT HERE.

09

Buffalo Bill packs a train w/
800 cowboys, 10 elk, 2 bear, Sitting Bull
& Annie Oakley w/ her strap-on pistols,
Ropes & ties them, spots god
In the snow-covered hills of Idaho—
Like a wildfire or a mining operation,
Entire landscapes can disappear—there are
Mountains missing near Wallace, Idaho &
Butte, Montana—there are burns
The size of a small east-coast state.

10

Dreams 3 nights in a row
Of riding the wild elk—
Fisting tines of sure antler,
Straddling the back, leaning in line
w/ its strong neck—
Tongue & spittle flying,
Bucking across a landscape of
Gold & sage—
The U.S. Cavalry
Arriving in a storm of dust.

11

Dale Evans, 1914-2001

What was it like riding Roy Rogers—
Did you dig his thighs w/ your spurs
As you galloped into Hollywood sunsets—
Whip his ass when he reared up
Down on all fours—cinch the saddle
A little tighter to let him know
Who was on top—did you bridle desires—
Harness hope—rope him in so he wouldn't
Buck you—one hand on the reins
The other circling a lasso?

12

Gregory Corso, 1930-2001

It's time to go, Gregory Corso,
Leave America & its imperfections
Behind—die while there's time
To believe you leave a democracy
Behind—status quo stole in
5 days after you turned your
Dark stare away from America—
Die & move to footnotes & alsos—
Resistance rests underground now
So go, Gregory Corso, just go.

13

Ken Kesey, 1935-2001

All the cliché & melted Dada-like
Steering wheel its mind blown again
Having to somehow deal—
Dropping & heading dead east I-90
Pursuing sunrise of day-glo Oregon
Going further—veers left
Into a Lewis & Clark rest area—
Always goofing
Always on the bus always
So damn merry.

14

Joey Ramone, 1951-2001

I saw U—Lake Ontario club—
1978—I was the one
Pogoing in back—spilling as
Much beer as I was drinking—
Genesee Cream Ale in green
Cans—U in ripped T-shirt—
Torn-knee jeans w/ guitar
On stage—I'd like to see U
Again—if you feel the same
Call me.

15

Upheaval
Teeth buckling
Like a cement viaduct lacking
Reinforcements—
Enamel peeling
Molars like brick from a building
Reclaiming bog—
Cheek puffing out
Tender abscess stressed
To fever pitch.

16

Beyond the curtain left open
Like the door of a birdcage
Spotlight & streetlight
Compete w/ neon light
On its night perch
Someone in the crowd
Yells "free bird"
On stage
She makes her best
Elvis move.

17

for Mark Andersen

Does she know what she does to this dog
There on the cover of long-playing vinyl
Wearing a fleshy slip w/ thin straps
She pulls her black hair back arms raised
Reveals this amazing underarm bush
O—
No airbrushing no commercial slickness
Arousing what lies beyond what's given
w/ a gesture so fine it redefines real
The power of her body as it is.

18

Vasectomy leaves the nuts, you know
It's not like a court eunuch
In China or a Montana
Testicle festival, nothing
Was served up on a platter
No—
You still wear pants,
Lap beer, sniff
French perfume,
Mark your territory w/ piss.

19

Richard Gilkey, 1925-1997

Mind sutras of mud greens
Float above flood plains
Severed heads of stained &
Yellow landscapes struggle
Like faked Sanskrit
Reeds bow to autumn agriculture
There's salt on the horizon
A bullet wound drips rust
Decay underlies each still life
Builds up like dust.

20

The simplest are the hardest
To describe—abstraction
Only looks easy—in fact
Calla lilies arrive w/
Broad green leaves—
At the center of still life
Their strong straight stalks
Unwrap—can only be thought of
As cupped & white—
Already all ready.

21

Philip Whalen, 1923-2002

"I'd like to be laid on a bed
Of frozen raspberries" you said
A few days before you were dead
Like some kind of crazy *koan*
That would unravel the mind-
Thoughts of those left behind
Pull the last loose thread
Of the wool from over our eyes
Let us see the absurdity of how
Seriously we take the dying.

22

Family & summer humidity
Get in your face—
This explains why Japanese chose
Typhoon weather to honor
Ancestral spirits—why they believe
Dead family members return the eighth
Month—why they build bonfires &
Sweep graves during the muggy season—
Why it keeps the bereaved honest &
Works the family into a sweat.

23

Oshujin sits on *zabuton*
In a tatami-matted room
Waits for sake to be poured
For him—*oii!* calls for rice
Gruel—*oii!*—2 times before
Passing out—futon folded
Behind paper doors is rolled
Out for him—he's covered
w/ thick blankets—next morning
Never once wonders what happened.

24

He doesn't go w/ the other men
To the pink salon—doesn't strip
Off work clothes & lie on a bench
w/ calloused hands behind his
Head—doesn't anticipate
The sliding door—the shuffle of a woman
In white terrycloth kimono—doesn't get
The hot-towel treatment nor the handjob—
Doesn't close his eyes & desire
He's somewhere, someone else.

25

Pigeons are urban buddhas
Plumped up
Jammed w/ sutras, cooing
Puffed, glittered, iridescent—
Not emaciated buddhas
Of sacrifice, but fleshed
& feathered—
Zazen on ledges above shops
Never telling when *satori*
Will drop.

26

Ken Furugori, 1930-2001

There's that damned bird again
Its crazy hoot-dee-hoot
It knows I'm in earshot
O—the emptiness
Low fronts bring to the Strait
Gray voids & blanked-out
Noons—
Summers shouldn't be this color—
I'm standing in the driveway ready to go
When through the cedars, that loon.

27

This boy's damn good
At keeping things in
Lived life below sea-level
His finger in the wall
Bit his lip to stop
A flood of unchained turrets
Teeter-tottered undiked
Between saving the day
Or giving up—
Then just pulled the plug.

28

This is a direct experience—spiritual
Existence is mandatory
Or we couldn't care
Less, couldn't impress
Indifference
Where the brown season
Leafless branches
Bow bent & barren
Outside
The arched window.

29

He believed he was preparing his body
For an accident, for blunt trauma
Or gunshot wound, hardening
For a hit, 4 more years of
Meanness & indifference,
Readying to pull himself from
Ruin, debris or rubble,
He'd be tough, know it
Could be tougher
As he pulls, lifts, stretches.

30

Close
Yet lost
As survey markers, unknown as
Who lives out back,
Domain demands
Attention to such details,
Your kitchen cupboards
Garages, silos
Ready to be
Emptied.

31

Why would you have a word for that
Moment when the sun crests
Mountain, halos the ridge line
w/ a horizontal brush
That now how wow moment—
How disappointing to sum
Enlightenment in one word
When it extends beyond
When in a moment
Covers much more than that.

32

I see Robert Creeley say
"American poetry is I-dependent"
& without irony pull a handkerchief
From his sleeve remove his glasses
& wipe the socket of his missing
Left eye—the very next morning
I overhear someone say "I think
You spend too much time on your eye"
& although it isn't really about Creeley
I see his I.

33

In April
Before lilacs
This bundle of sticks
w/ purple-veined
Leaves waits—
In the shade
On the north side
The septic side of the house
Pants down
Ass bared—waits.

34

Beneath maples
Not yet leafed
He points
& pisses—
Flash of sun
A golden arc
Darkens bark
In widening streaks—
Stains winter grasses
w/ his mark.

35

He copies the words to "Heroin"
From the liner notes on the sleeve
Of the Velvet Underground LP—
Signs his name in pencil—
Leaves the lyrics on the kitchen table
w/ a note
Erases that he loves her he's always loved her—
In the pantry shakes
The last pennies from her
Peanut-butter jar.

36

It’s strange to think of
Sacajawea
At a bed & breakfast
But the sign says
She slept here
& in the morning
Didn’t say a thing
Used sign language
To order toast & coffee
Before she hit the trail.

37

for Lou Reed

The next morning
Master gets
Breakfast in bed
Confesses
He doesn't recall
What he did
Last night
Though the sense
Of new leather lingers
In the sheets.

38

You see a man carrying a 2x4
He's walking straight at you—you
Think—"it's all kind of random"—
Or you're in your car—you approach
An intersection—you see something out
Of the corner of your eye—you think
"It's just physics"—you think "it's
Hard to live moment-to-moment"—
You walk under a power line—
A crow dives at your head.

39

for John Ward

Gone—precisely—surgically—gone
Like the impression in
The cushion of the waiting room
Couch—shifting—
Restructuring—
What procedure leaves behind
& what it takes—what it
Lives without—
Standing—
A body remembering itself.

40

Too early for equinox
Late for orphanage
She pulls on yellow
Playtex gloves rags
The dust built up
Sweeps & resweeps
The floors the front porch
Relentlessly
Weeds & weeds
The garden.

41

march to the INS Building, Seattle, 2003.02.15

The river cuts a new channel
Through bog
Undermines
Floods 5th & Pike
A wash of slogans & graffiti
Changes the edges
Assembles a new corps
Footholds too tentative
To build on
The city shifting on its banks.

42

Tonight he is a poet—
Listening to jazz on the car radio
Snapping his fingers—he's a beatnik
Hep cat cool dude hip-hop man—
Driving the coast at midnight—caffeinated
Neverminding 9-to-5—
Improvising—he's a free-
Styling saxman
Blowing words—
Yes!

43

Joe Strummer, 1952-2002

Sax echoes
Through the underground—
There was a line
Drawn—
We always knew
What side to take—
On the street
The player blows
Each
Note—

44

Patti Smith, Moore Theater, Seattle, 2004.08.15

Stand up
Stand up
Stand up
Stand up
Stand up
Stand up
Stand up
Stand up
Stand up
Stand up!

45

He's a shoveler shovels
Dirt from one side of the yard
To the other—when he's done
He shovels it back where it came
From & starts again—a new
Century dirt farmer prepared
For the new depression—
Shovels without
Encouragement
Without regret.

46

Feast your eyes, Li Jin—
Plate, spoons & chopsticks
Platters of whole fish, pig
Heads, chicken feet,
Watercolors
Spilled on banquet table
Covered w/ yesterday's
Newspaper—spreading
Desire like a sauce
Hunger in your eyes.

47

June Carter Cash, 1929-2003

Not so much love but a flood—
Not desire touch skin
Not intimate but a river—
Not body mind heart
But current awash
A carrying away—
Not forgive-forget reunion
Not meet again someday—not
Second-hand second-time around
But this moment nothing but.

48

The night we were baptized under
The Aurora Bridge came unexpectedly—
Splashed over guardrail by passing
Vehicle indifferent to karma
Tsunami'd—wet *satori* sloshed
From heaven's floor onto our heads—once
We stood beneath the veranda
At Kiyomizu Temple in Kyoto—catching holy
Water in long-handled tin cups
As it rained gulps of blessing.

49

This constant lifting—
A generation
Constructs meaning
From what's found—
Knows history
To destroy
History—
Infrastructure &
Instruction
Fill landfills.

50

photograph of Rimbaud at Harar

A ghost a
Reluctant angel
Looks directly
Arms crossed
Cropped hair
Looks military
Dark blank stare
Wears a white
Tunic that flares
His slight waist.

51

William Burroughs, 1914-1997

What a cut-up
& that crack
In your voice
Matter-of-fact
Manual typewriter
Clack-clack-clack
Live long & lo
Folks make
Folk heroes
Out of outriders.

52

Ronald Reagan, 1911-2004

May your heart be blacker
Your indifference be skewered
May you be publicly
Ridiculed always
Be haunted by
Huddled masses
May your legacy unravel
Your remains be vilified
& on your grave be
Continuous pissing.

53

Arthur "Killer" Kane, 1949-2004

Stone solid planted
In the arms of sweet
Jesus—among stacks
Pumps of pimps
A kiss—a pluck
Constructs
Bottom-line
Heartthrobs—
On this stage
This angel still.

54

Hunter S. Thompson, 1937-2005

What a blast!
Your last trip
I mean mayhem
Wild Turkey
& Nixon's mob
Someone bit your
Finger for chrissake!
Pharmaceuticals
Spilt on floor
That peacock scream!

55

She said she already knew
Had known for a while &
Had already said it aloud
To him who admonished
Her not to ask but to wait
Until she told us herself
When she told us in her voice
It was better than listening
To silence than left to wonder
How she feels who she loves.

56

Close enough almost
To touch although
In separate space
To hear you in our hallway
Telltale floorboards steps
You try not to take
To sense you near
As you pass & pace
Cigarette smoke
Ghosting.

57

Dream 2007.03.10

From the shelter doorway
A landscape of cedar & fir
Signs that the ground is tidal—
A bear on the periphery
Her snout wet each
Facial bristle glistens
A sense of nearness
In each breath—
Shotgun on the wall
Just out of reach.

58

Dream 2010.01.25

Bear skin
Edges of sinew
& membrane
He stepped into the hind legs pulled
Broad fur hump onto his back
Covered his face w/ fitted
Skull
His arms filled
Its front legs
& crouched on all fours & ran off.

59

to Sam Hamill

Voice rising
Far end of
The woods
Simply saying
"Bullshit"
Sound of
A pebble
Tossed
Into a
Pond.

60

to José Kozer

My desperado
Along borderlands
In diaspora
Dispersed—
A conquistador
Taking this
Amorous land
By force—
My little refugee
Awash & awash.

61

for bill bissett

CANT READ UR
THOTS U-NO
SO LEAVE
MESSAGE RE
WHATS IN UR
HED WHAT U
R THINKING +
I-L LISTEN
VIA SPKR PHONE
2 UR DESIRES.

62

Daniel Johnston, 1961-2019

Talk into
My microphone
Let me hear
You say “I
LOVE YOU”
On my cassette recorder
I will dupe it
A hundred times
Give it away for
FREE.

63

Robin Blaser, 1925-2009

You weren't wanted here anyhow &
You haven't been missed for years
No one is quite sure what you've been up to
Up there
Canada
You must have been too busy to call &
No one here has written for months now
You'll never understand us why we can't
See the trees
See the forest.

64

Priscilla Maynard, 1921-2009

In the heart of the woods there is
A magical bamboo grove which isn't
Invasive of the neighbor's yard
(Angering the neighbor) but instead grows
Nourishing shoots & long tender panda
Leaves—what makes it magical is its
Shades of sumi: cloud-covered gray
Brush-stroked black & (this uninked
Area being the most critical to the entire
Composition) empty-space nothing.

65

Jim Carroll, 1950-2009

Pure as
Skyscrapers
Of Mannahatta
High heels
On Times Square
Condoms drifting
In East River
A midtown god
On the nod
Punk clouds.

66

Michael Doubles, 1953–2009

The last time we were together
Your body my body roomed
In this town of motels &
Marquee moons & intersections
Banded together in crazy
Jazz-time continuum
Moments in physicality or
As poet-friend Jed says
What presence will remain
In the flux of our lives.

67

Michael Doubles, 1953–2009

Sound the alarm
Start the evacuation
Move w/ purpose
Toward the EXIT
Hide out
In stairwell echo
End that kiss
Press your lips
To horn to
"Blow, bugle, blow."

68

How the body embodies the soul
How the soul equals the poem
The poetics of the body all parts
Of the body all functions of the body
Writes on the soul a poem
The width & breadth of the body
The measure of the poem
The physicality of the soul
On our souls on our bodies
Soulful body language.

69

for Evan Flory-Barnes

His hands all over
The low notes he
Finds the bottom
That which is base
Vibrational/elemental
His own string theory
Strikes a note
Resonates souls/soles
That keep beat
Like hearts.

70

Methinks I have mistaken
Methinks this matter
Methinks my body
Methinks faith a jackal
Methinks things are not
Without their meaning
As if each
Silence
Insular & incommunicable
Methinks old wounds.

71

There is
Magic in it
Such a mystical
Such a portentous
Monster
Carries you
Infallibly
Leading you
To over-
Whelming.

72

for JT Stewart

Listen to waves
To sailing out
To paddles of
Disbelief the distance
You put before me
Listen to the breaks
The hard times "our
Own emotions will scare
Us shitless" listen
To that.

73

Peter Orlovsky, 1933-2010

Keep your asshole clean
& your vegetables singing
Merrily along—
Stand bare-chested
Among garden blooms
Up puckered moons
Boozily rolling along—
Care for your brother
In opening swoon
Lovingly tenderly along.

74

Flap
Flap
Flap
Flap
Flap
Flap
Flap
Flap
Flap
Flap.

75

for Martin Appleby

I stick my head thru the jukebox
& think about anarchists in black
As if Johnny wasn't my real name
As peacocks scream & scream
I can tell by the junk in their throats
All the tear gas & all the meaning
I'll rip my shirt & wave my flag
But when this song is finished
I'm going to leave this bar
My angel wings sprouting early.

76

Keep me on a short leash
My throat to your hand
Beaten & collared
Watch me mark
My territory
Survey the perimeter
Mapped by your chaining
Hear my beagled moans
Thru leather muzzle
My choked desires.

77

Sid Vicious, 1957-1979

I believe in anarchy
In apathy
In cuts & scars
In redneck bars
In padlocks
& submission
In what we did
In fucked up &
Fuck you—
I believe in Sid.

78

It rains all night awake
You hear drumming
On canvas you see
Nothing yet sense
Desire a river
Emptying into ocean you
Taste dampness of rot
Your clothes soaked
Your nostrils flare
w/ lingering salt.

79

Patti Smith, The W, Seattle, 2010.01.25

Lean close
Speak softly
Into her ear
Offer gifts to her
Talismans in
Buttoned silk
Creased Polaroids w/
Scalloped edges
At her gate
Leave drums.

80

Owsley "Bear" Stanley, 1935-2011

w/ these hands
w/ this mind
w/ 5 million hits of
Acid—
A head ahead of
His time unbound
By organic rewiring
By new consciousness
Head-on into eternal
Wall-of-sound.

81

Samples: Alan Lau, Francine Sedars Gallery, 2011.04.20

What remains after
Music stops
"I'm late again"
What's inside
A pagoda of art
"I remember you"
Saxophone blows
"Chinatown"
What sound do
Onion skins make.

82

@ Highway 99 Blues Club

Hit it
Hit it
Hit it
Hit it
Hit it
Hit it
Hit it
Hit it
Hit it
Hit it.

83

Lawrence Ferlinghetti, 1919-2021

Stood on edge
Americus stage
Shouted decades
Recited
From memory
What has passed—
Looked out on streets
Renamed—took
Direction from Old
Whitman's beard.

84

Lawrence Ferlinghetti, 1919-2021

To stand 100+1 years
To not yield
To advocate & build
To double down
To occupy war-weary town
To front revolution after
Revolution after revolution
To spin that karma wheel
To fly off like crow
Across sumi-washed sky.

85

Diane di Prima, 1934-2020

May I call you goddess
Ye who enters me
Fornicates my mind
Absolves all thoughts—
May I call you wolf
Ye who devours me
Leaves this carcass
Exposed & castrated—
May I tend your garden
May I mend your hem?

86

Michael McClure, 1932-2020

Leave blank
What's blank
Find your center
Let edges be edges
Take what starts
As an idea as
Ink to brush
& give it breath
w/ one stroke—
Birth to death.

87

Joanne Kyger, 1934-2017

I know what you're saying
That I have to see
What's right in front of me
& not set sights
On distant desires
I must get by
w/ my own eyes—
From time to time
Spot in the alley
Coyote passing by.

88

"No it was no dream of coming death"—Zukofsky

Pissing in the woods
Is the closest I come
To accepting Christ
As my personal savior—
I count trees
Pace off the distance
To where your stones
Are stacked—
Others kneel but
I stay standing.

89

Sleater-Kinney @Showbox, 2015.05.08

How can I stand here—
Power has shifted—
The message
Has been amplified—
The banner unfurled—
Bricks have been hurled
Thru glass—
Obscurity smashed
Leaving shards in
My kicked ass.

90

Give me that mic
& I will shout
Let everyone else
Be screamed out
What do you care if
I won't shut up
You'll have to
Pull the plug
Says this punk poet
To make me stop.

91

My body
Your body
All bodies fail—
To be no body
SO WHAT—
It's flesh
It's touch
It's desire—
Says this punk poet
"Go, just go."

92

It was your guitar
That first bit me
Before eating
My ears
Before I felt
Your tongue
Lick my mind
That chewed
10 times before
I was swallowed.

93

Oh my god
Do you really
Expect me
To prostrate
To be covered w/ dirt
To always look up
To look you in the eye
Says this punk poet
Who spits & whom
Gets spit on?

94

Tell me
Who will be left
For you to destroy—
Our bunkers bombed
Our flesh assaulted—
We who remain
Remain as refugees—
Soon there will be
None of us left
Says this punk poet.

95

Burn, America, burn
Dry up & burn
Burn w/ outrage
& hatred burn
These streets burn
These houses
These woods
Burn every damned thing
Burn desire
Burn even this.

96

I dreamt the street
Was empty except
For charred remains
Of a police cruiser—
I had the sense someone
Was watching me
Thru closed blinds—
There were no dogs
No one to help me
Name this feeling.

97

I dreamt I was a junkie
I had a dull needle
Stuck in my arm
After I pulled it out
I didn't know what
To do w/ the syringe—
There was a dark pond
w/ drifting shiftless
Lotus blossoms that
Lacked direction too.

98

What do you know of desire
Scent of desiccation
Or lingering
Musk of sweat-soaked
Pillow—fish
Deboned of their flesh
Left in unformed piles
For desire's rankness
To become known
Seeped in ferment.

99

Like Johnny Thunders
I'm aware enough
To wear a dress
Dance for you
Drunken & drugged
But never a drag
(You know the rest)
Talented, misunderstood
I won't be canonized
Until I'm dead.

100

WHOEVER
TOOK MY
BLONDIE LPs
PLEASE
RETURN
THEM—
NO
QUESTIONS
ASKED—
I FORGIVE U.

17 VIEWS OF MOUNT FUJI

For everybody on the bus when we circumnavigated Mount Fuji, 1988.08.13

Input from "100 Views of Mount Fuji" by ukiyo-e artist Hokusai

01

Look—
You can't be a buddha by reading a book—
You can't know Mount Fuji from *ukiyoe* prints
Or travel brochures—
It's not as you imagine—not snow-capped
Pine-framed meditative but sudden
Ashen & low—a *kabuki* actor
Without make-up—not obvious despite
All the views—you won't know it at first—
Only a break in the clouds.

02

In *ukiyoe* prints—people—
If depicted at all—are
Almost always insignificant to
Landscape—painted in
A corner—doing mundane
Things—when you first see
Mount Fuji from the road
You won't remember
Who is driving or where
You are going.

03

It's raining still—the thatched roof
Leaks a little—the family has built
A new house but she stays
Here—squats among the dust
& photos (says she was always
Better w/ her mouth
Than her hands)
In the middle of the hallway
Between the floorboards—
A bamboo shoot.

04

in memory, Noriko Haruta

Progress needs stillness—
She studies moments
In dance the stops—
She knows each expression
Leads—
The blur of motion
Interprets backgrounds—
Like mountains
She knows things last—
Things don't.

05

The baths at Hakone—
Spewing spit & bile
(Hidden inner passion)
Tubbed & channeled
Lit cemented ionized
Boiling steaming—
Quickly sketched
Visitors in *yukata* & slippers
Between soakings
Robed (like Fuji).

06

Ukiyoe "floating world pictures"
Can be read "pictures of everyday life"—
Uki to rise or float to the surface—*yo* the world
Or generations—& *e* picture—*ukiyo*
The transitory world
Or as a buddha says "all things impermanent &
Uncertain"—the moment
You realize the bus isn't going to the sea
But turns inland
Toward the mountain.

07

The Fujicolor overlook
Is perfect—top third
Of white-blue clouds & mountain—
The center greens of paddies
& bamboo—the bottom third
The foreground people (nearly
Not there) pose
& (although
The picture taker doesn't move) Mount Fuji
Appears & disappears frame by frame.

08

Watch live internet cam 24-hour-a-day
Mount Fuji—watch night
Shadows cross like *sumi*
Drying—watch town lights die
At midnight—sunrise red like Tokyo
Fire-bombed—boats wave
On the bay—or watch nothing—
Fog—clouds—rain—
A single drop on the lens—
A daily life.

09

In one Hokusai print
There are no people
No sign of people
Only the summit above blackness
Slashed w/ red lightning
What's below
No one imagines
A wash of white
The way our eyes
Mound toward heaven.

10

287 stone steps 7 flights
To reach Nichiren temple grounds—
We count 41-1 … 41-2 … it's a game …
41-3 … then we know … 41-4 …
We're going to die … 41-5 ... we
Lose count … 41-6 or 41-7 …
Before the raked heaven ... ah—
The temple grounds
Where our aunt (who got a ride up the back way)
Greets us w/ an orange.

11

The way
Narrows—
The bus crawls past steep terraced
Fields—past temples & lakes—
Volcanic rocks hidden—waterfalls
w/ warning signs—"Don't Work In" —
While in the back of the bus
We drink Budweiser from cans
Too close
To Fuji to see the summit.

12

(Didn't climb Mount Fuji)
Sometimes it's better
To imagine you did—
Desire lasts longer
Than pictures
& postcards—
Keeps things
You want the most
Exactly the way
You want them.

13

in memory, Toshikatsu Kusakari

Looking up *fuji* in the dictionary
There are 4 readings—
(1) wisteria (2) all alone
(3) untimely &
(4) incurable or hopeless—
Fuji faces winter all alone—
Wisteria in full bloom hangs from
The tea house—perfumes death—
When the phone rings
It's tomorrow in Japan.

14

Not two—one—facing the wave—*ronin*
One rowing in the storm—off Kanagawa—
Waves that rise & fall below
Summit & sunrise—the ocean
Ranks things—our view
Of work—of passing through the world—
A perfect *enso* wave can toss a boat around
At will—that the rower keeps rowing—
From Hokusai's perspective—
A wave taller than Mount Fuji.

15

Still not sure—
A swatch at the peripheral
Lapping the edge where
Things are unclear—where
Land erodes—microfilms in
Dream retinas—this color—
Buoyant—floats routine—
Unanchors footings
Of arbitrary
Tugged tides of green.

16

Mount Fuji cannot be a postcard—cannot be
An icon—cannot be the colors
Of a still life (a photo
Doesn't last longer)
Ukiyoe cannot be the everyday
Driving bus—drinking beer—
Stopping this moment to pray or piss—
Cannot impress colors on a heart
The untimely deaths we die—the way
We carry on.

17

w/ each reproduction
Colors fade—
Black & white Mount
Fuji—green shoots of
Bamboo—purple
Blossomed wisteria—
The red fire
In ideas & desire—
(Mountain & mind erode)
See.

INCIDENT AT YELLOWSTONE

A Montana tale in 10 pieces from the fall of '83 wherein a camper is mauled to death by a grizzly bear

01

Form is not for the weak of heart
What holds us together magnetizes
Our atoms, pulls closer
Pushes farther apart

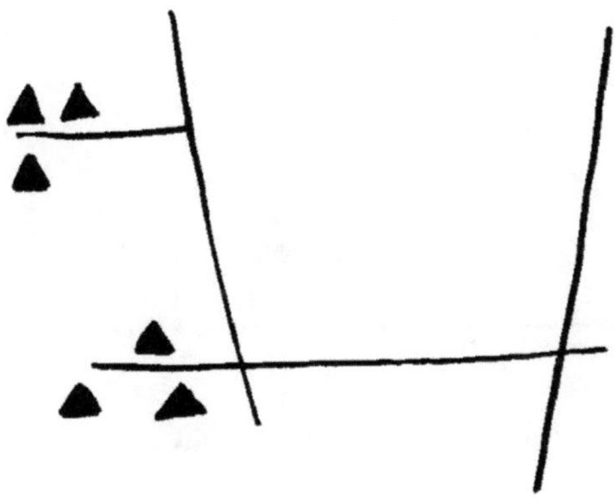

02

Intersections appear straight
But they're a tangle

2 cross paths at the same
Place, the same time, take
The same turn

End up in the same camp

03

Stillness deep as the lake
As quiet as Mackinaw
As meaningless as the flat
Surface

There is no moon

A circle of stones, embers
A Ford
A tent among the pines

04

Somewhere peripheral a branch snaps

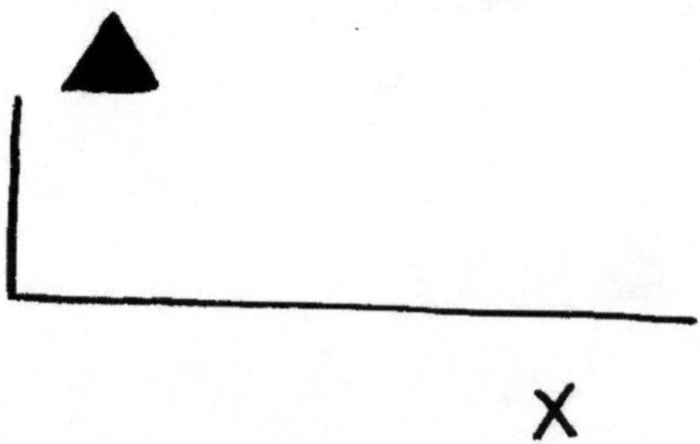

05

When the she-bear comes around
She finds a tent
Swipes through nylon
Catches him in the head
Drags him, rolls him
Around & around

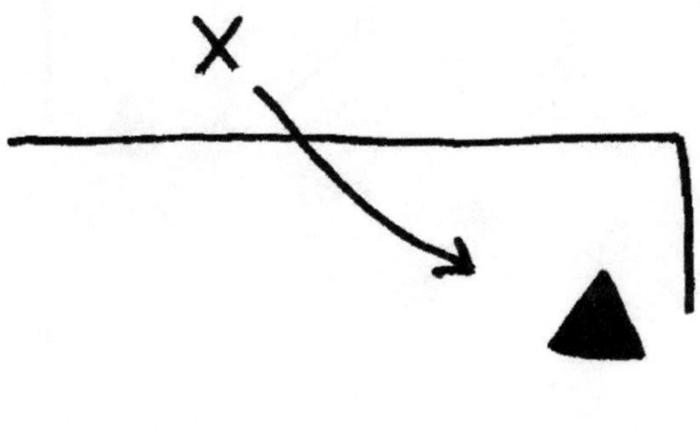

06

One minute asleep, the next not
One minute dreaming, the next not

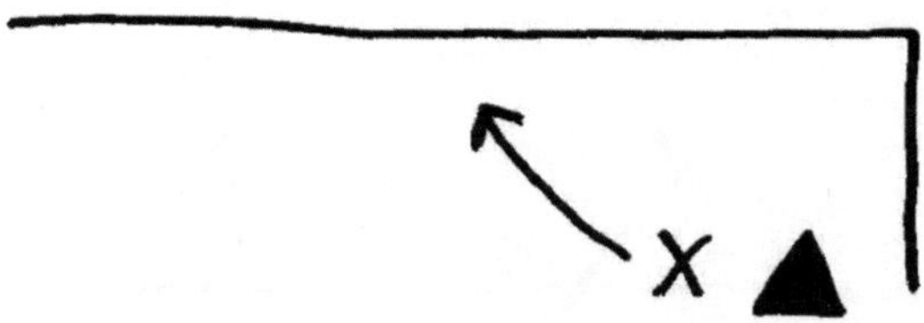

07

If you saw the pieces you'd say
It doesn't make sense

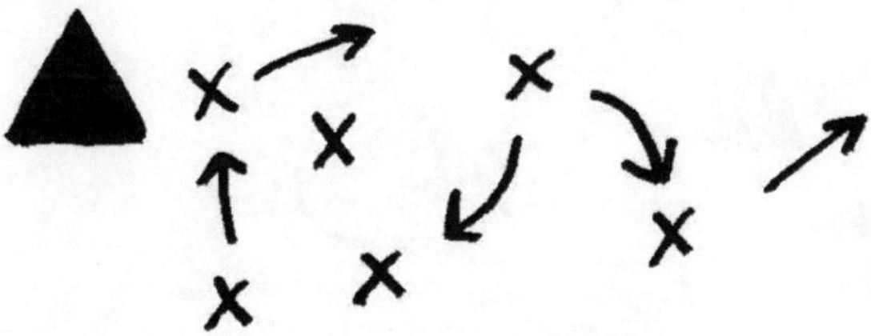

08

Sheriff arrives on the scene
Shines a light on lodgepoles
Illuminates a trail
A snapped branch, blood
An intersection

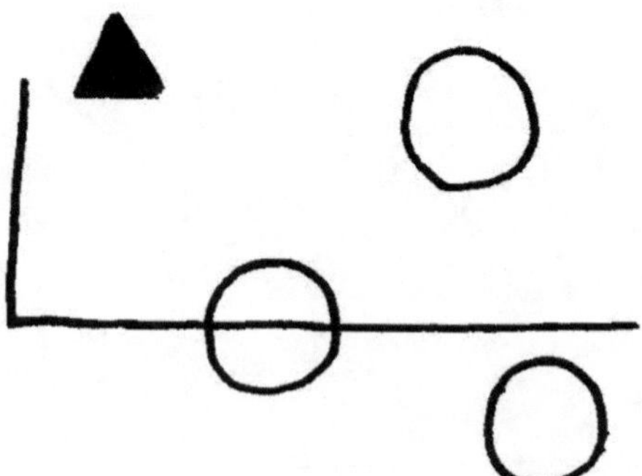

09

It takes physics
To set a trap
Detachment
To place a rib in a plastic bag

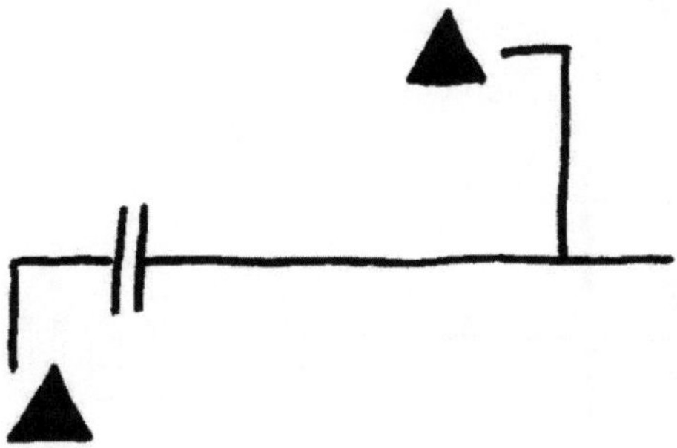

10

Waking w/ a hangover
You accept things the way they are
You get going

The challenge has always been
To put things together again

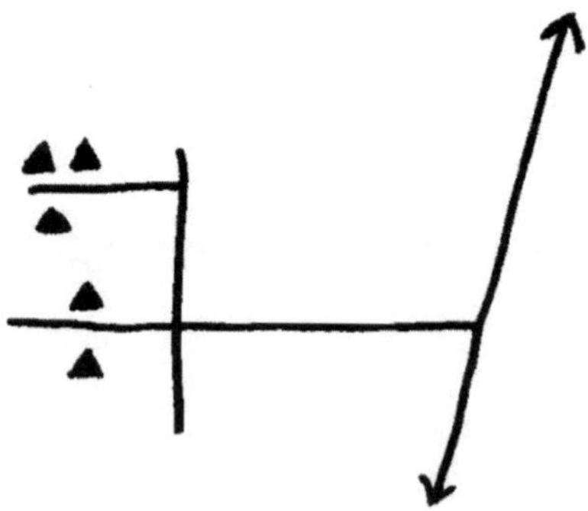

10 IMPERFECT SONNETS

The adjacent mountains commonly rise so high
as to conceal the more distant & lofty mountains
from our view. –Meriwether Lewis, 1805.07.24

01

Could I love her more if she wore dark glasses &
A scarf like Jackie O—if she chain-smoked, spit &
Swore, shot back whiskey, bucked like a bronco—
If she spoke of disappointment, lived a landscape
Of bare light bulbs & ashtrays, broke hearts, sang
Of redemption, desire, escape—if she made me
Wear a dog collar, sit up & wait for her at the kitchen
Table—if she called me Daddy when she came in late
As if we were both longing to find out
What Hank Williams was talking about.

02

Patsy Cline's singing on the jukebox Sunday night
How love lingers like smoke from cigarettes left
Burning in ashtrays or ice cubes at the bottom
Of a whiskey-coke—how love sticks around like
Red lipstick on a shirt or a shot glass & you're
Missing love even more than Saturday night
When you left him lying split-lipped
Flat out on the barroom floor
Face-down in peanut shells & spilt beer
Curled-up bloodied like a newborn steer.

03

"I have the kiss of Walt Whitman's still on my lips."
–Oscar Wilde

Is it that "I love you" is too trite
That it's too short, too few words
That a mouth can't take it seriously
Is it too easily lied, a tongue slipping
On its consonants, or does it have too
Much teeth & grinds commitment—I say
Let atoms attract, let our lips
Speak for flesh on flesh
Let I's single electron fly to
The soft round pucker of you.

04

I don’t remember when I stopped sleeping
When I started simply keeping busy &
Going to bed when it was still light out
But not sleeping even w/ the lights out
Dreaming something about a bear
How much I admired her instinct sleeping
Through half a life—if only I could
Stay in bed—hibernate—not dreaming—
Let vacuuming wait until April
Let dust build up where it will.

05

I need love like D.B. Cooper love
The kind you strap on before you jump
Miles above a hijacked landscape—
You find on a river bank
Tangled like a bomber jacket
In salal or blackberry—you
Read about front page says lived
Incognito in Portland for years—
Love you can't apprehend
Once the chute has opened.

06

You too punk will age—too soon
Blemishes which neon conceals
Will glare at noon—like stares
A man in heels gets, just try
To hide desires dragged out
Midday—you too will suit up
Dress for day jobs, grow way
Too fat, too entrenched, too taxed
Way too satisfied
Fit to be tied.

07

John Morris Catchman, 1914-1978

Some things he'll never be forgiven for—some
Things not forgotten—some things become
Opaque—the color of home-brew—some
Set up in his gut like cement—sometimes
She wonders why he never learned to pray—
Never let Jesus come—some Sundays
He gets his fiddle out & she can almost
Forgive him—forget
The tunes he plays & she can't place—
"That Lonesome Whistle," "Amazing Grace."

08

Bill must have loved the buffalo—the way
They added great brown humps
To the low-rolling monotony of landscape—
The way they stampeded like Cavalry
Recruits or dancehall wives not afraid
Of hard rides—O—what he must have
Desired—when he set his sights—fired—
Notched his belt for each one bedded
w/ a husband's sure aim—
He even took their name.

09

Since you left I've been as lonely
As a Johnny Cash song solitary
As a man without parole
No more appeal
I've been as sad as
A train at 4 a.m.
Pawned my wedding band
For an acoustic guitar
Strummed "Ring of Fire" learned to rhyme
Earned my forgiveness, a song at a time.

10

O—if I had to live off the land
Move dirt from one side of the field
To the other—dam muddy streams
To irrigate dry crops—returning
Return to the land—work 100 days
Without a day's rest—mend fences
Pull barbed wire—keep an eye out for
That chicken thief who wants what's mine—
Know how to persevere
Hammer & shotgun near.

FOR THE RECORD

Uncollected Poems, 1999-2005

FOR THE RECORD

we are like that car
I walk by parked on Thomas Street
its back seat and passenger side crammed
with papers, books, magazines, newspapers
and atop this heap of memory scrap pile
                    waits
a 2.5-gallon can of gasoline

King County Poetry + Art On Buses, 1999

UPON READING BUKOWSKI

maybe it's because
I've been reading
Bukowski
lately but
I reek of gasoline
the way
alcohol seeps
from your skin
after drinking too much
I'm sweating gasoline
the smell
burns my nostrils
I'm afraid
to light a match

a friend says
Bukowski's dead you know
every time I mention

Bukowski
someone tells me he's dead
but how
did he die
was he soaked too
when he lit that match

PoetsWest Literary Journal, 1999

WALKING PAST A MORRIS GRAVES RETROSPECT

dead sea bird
clear-cut landscape
scraped & shaped
with a painter's knife
until raw brown canvas
shows through
thin white scratch down the center
splits the gray-browns
the mud-greens, the black skies
wounded brant
decapitated horse
harvested spring leeks
half-ripped panels salvaged
from the brown hills of Hollywood
(Hepburn's estate)
sometimes a gentle, thin-stalked flower
insignificant red blossoms surrounded

by charred blacks, burnt rubble
black washes of sumi
dead birds
gas masks
bronze vessels, Ming Dynasty, China
the center line
the mad Tobey-esque squiggles
"bird caught in moonlight"
tangled in geometry
struggles against abstraction
it all ends in a single brush stroke
a bird
brown rice paper awash in gray
"gauche & sumi on paper"
a white line
a bird
in just one stroke
satori
a bird

PoetsWest Literary Journal, 1999

FIRE ON THE HANFORD NUCLEAR RESERVATION

Our first sign: a burning bush

left to extinguish itself
not 30 feet off the road

we see radioactive tumbleweeds
charred & tangled in barbed wire

the sun choked and filtered
Apocalyptic by plutonium smoke

after the War we are tourists
detoured by Toppenish firefighters

down an empty 6-lane highway past
unoccupied parking lots & billboards

"Welcome to Hanford
Where Safety Comes First"

we follow railroad tracks
past spent shells of boxcars

& end up at the Visitors'Center
for Production Plant #2 on the wrong day

greeted by a yellow warning sign:
"No Public Access"

we find where the line's been drawn
where sides have been taken in desert

while all around us
the Wasteland Battleground blazes

the core red of meltdown

PoetsWest Literary Journal, 2000

THEN I CATCH MYSELF SITTING

Then I catch myself sitting
Across the room from you
Off by my lunar self again
The silence
Between us
Enough space for
A meteor shower
Later in our bedroom
I open the blinds to
Let the moonlight in.

4th Street, 2001

ALL THE IMAGES FROM THIS WAR WILL BE IN GREEN

(a)
All the images from this war will be in green
Goggled visions, manipulated streams of video
Punctured bursts that nova'd light years ago
But we're only seeing now—infrared shadows
Linger in retinas even w/ our eyes averted—
Like campaign slicks of body parts wrapped
In the colors of the day (in peacetime it's
Advertising, in wartime it's propaganda)
A culture triggered by media blitzes
Will buy & buy until it's sold.

(b)
But what can we learn from birds
Dark flocks across cement skies
Huddled but not touching
Reactive flitters of nerves

Using song instead of piss
To mark their territories
Refugees packing for the border
Heading south in autumnal descent
Like we don't believe winter's near
Like we don't believe what we hear.

PoetsWest Literary Journal, 2002

HOMELAND SECURITY

Bring me swing me
Do that thing you do to me
Homeland Security

Beat me then talk sweet to me
You know how to treat me
Homeland Security

Handcuff me act tough with me
I love it when you're rough with me
Homeland Security

Report me deport me
Stop the import of more like me
Homeland Security

You found me now impound me
Go ahead round up all like me
Homeland Security

Shoot me loot me blindfold me
& gag me to mute me
Homeland Security

Inundate me sedate me make me
Believe only update TV gives me
Homeland Security

Alarm me disarm me
Just don't let them harm me
Homeland Security

Wiretap me cause a flap
Until nerves finally snap on me
Homeland Security

Lie to me spy on me
Better keep your eye on me
Homeland Security

www.poetsagainstthewar.org, 2003 + Pontoon, 2004

GO AHEAD & CROW ROOSTER

Go ahead & crow rooster—but we're not getting
Out of bed today—you can insist with your
Alarmist horning—but we're not letting
Love leave these downy sheets—no—your
Banter won't rouse these hearts—we
Don't care that 2 blocks east Aurora waits
Or that sun's interrogation will soon be
Unblocked from mountains' shadows—gates
Of dawn flung open—your cock-a-doodle-do—
Your manly cackle—won't open our eyes
To any such glare—so do what you have to do—
But we won't stop dreaming—we will not rise—
Your morning can turn to noon,
We're waiting for the moon.

Cranky Literary/Arts Journal, 2004

UPRISING (GUANTANAMO BAY)

O baby under boots faked suicide
surveillance electric shock chains
hooded examiners cubist landscape
our hearts prison iron that will not bend

when it rains from the ground up, 2005

ADVICE FOR THE NEXT GENERATION OF PUNKS

for Jack and Aya
for Eliot, Emiko, and Powell

Be high Whitmans.

Be old-maid Dickinsons.

Fear no gods.

Live with the fact you are singular souls left alone to
ponder the cruel ironies of your existential existence.
You are Sartre, you are Camus on a bad acid trip.

Learn the lessons of Walden Pond. Live off your
friends' land. Grow your own. Avoid your neighbors.
Transcend accidentally.

Don't think insurance salesmen can't be great poets. Contractors of the imagination, suited saints of the cubicles, Wallace Stevenses on the time clock can write too.

Ban the phrase "day job" from your vocabulary. Concentrate on the real work.

It's stupid to write a 500-word essay about white chickens next to a red wheelbarrow.

Ignore the fact bumper stickers and soundbites are the new poetic yardsticks.

If you can't say it in 3 minutes you need a good editor.

Point things out "directly, purely, concretely, no abstractions, no explanations."

Agree "first thought, best thought."
Read Blake, read Ginsberg.

Use a manual typewriter. Spontaneous bop prose in all its beatific prosaic mosaic beauty doesn't work on a word processor.

Don't end up old Bull Lees shooting heroin in Mexico City or pop cans in Kansas City.

Be Patti Smith holy, Jim Carroll pure, Lou Reed wise.

Remember: To just say no is to never know.

Whatcom Poetry Series: The Poet As Art; broadside by Egress Studio Press, 2005

This book is number 66 of 125

TO JUST SAY NO
IS TO NEVER KNOW

JB

ACKNOWLEDGMENTS

Thanks to the editors who first published some of these punk poems in *4th Street, Cranky Literary Journal, elimae, Gumball Poetry, King County Poetry and Art on Buses, Poetry at Parkplace Books, Poetry International, Poets Against the War, PoetsWest Literary Journal, Pontoon, Real Change, Snow Monkey, Whatcom Poetry Series.*